MIRACLES HAPPENS EVERYDAY

7 STEPS

of

MANIFESTATION

Ruchi Rai

BLUEROSE PUBLISHERS
India | U.K.

Copyright © Ruchi Rai 2025

All rights reserved by author. No part of this publication may be reproduced, stored in a retrieval system or transmitted in any form or by any means, electronic, mechanical, photocopying, recording or otherwise, without the prior permission of the author. Although every precaution has been taken to verify the accuracy of the information contained herein, the publisher assumes no responsibility for any errors or omissions. No liability is assumed for damages that may result from the use of information contained within.

BlueRose Publishers takes no responsibility for any damages, losses, or liabilities that may arise from the use or misuse of the information, products, or services provided in this publication.

For permissions requests or inquiries regarding this publication, please contact:

BLUEROSE PUBLISHERS
www.BlueRoseONE.com
info@bluerosepublishers.com
+91 8882 898 898
+4407342408967

ISBN: 978-93-6261-154-3

Cover design: Yash Singhal
Typesetting: Namrata Saini

First Edition: March 2025

May miracles happen every day in your life & transform the lives of those reading this book, miracles happen when you count the miracles, and I am sure this book will transform your life to happiness, abundance, and good health.

I want to show my sincere gratitude to the universe, which helped me become a life coach to transform millions of people through this book, from my childhood I looked up to the sky. I always asked the universe to give me some power like that of superman in movies or serials who suddenly comes and help the person who needs the help. Talking to people was my passion from childhood, listen to their problems, and guide them in the best possible way was my passion, but that was not enough, one day I realized god had given me something special, and that was my positive thought, positive outlook towards life & that is my powerful tool, through which I can help other, by motivating them for positive thinking. I also became a professional numerologist by reading about numbers, started using my psychic power to heal someone's problem by numerology, and used my intuition, but the power working behind me is only the almighty god universe, which helps me help otherss. So, it's all because of the universe. But I manifested my desire to help someone, so now I am helping people through numerology and also by life coaching for manifesting their desire. So thank you universe for manifesting my desire.

I also want to show sincere gratitude to my father B.D. Rai thank you papa, actually, I learnt the manifestation technique from my father in my childhood, but at that time I was not aware of the word manifestation, the thing I know only what my father mostly speaks, which I will tell you in the later part of this book. But really that worked, because I was a deep thinker from my childhood, I saw & observed him very well, so now I can relate to it, that it was manifestation & he became the owner of zero to a rich self made man. And I am writing this book because of my father, he never stops me from doing anything, he always encourages me to do, whatever I want to do. And his belief in me is my biggest motivation.

I want to show my gratitude to all my teachers, thank you because of them I got a lot of knowledge, and now I am able write this book.

I want to thank my husband for his support for all the things I needed to write this book. Also thank you to all my family members for their support.

I want to thank my daughter, for her unconditional love, which is my biggest power to do something unconditionally. I am writing this book to share unconditional love and blessings.

I want to thank all the team members who helped me to write this book, to transform millions of people's lives around the world .

Lastly, I want to thank myself, who keeps the intention to transform millions of people's lives through this book

CONTENTS

Miracles Happens Everyday 1
Words Have Power 5
What Your Emotion Speaks 8
Forgiveness 12
Self-Love 15
Clarity of Thought and Belief 20
Visualization 26
Let's Create the Miracles 30
A story 44

MIRACLES HAPPENS EVERYDAY

(Count the miracle)

Here I want to share the stories of miracles that I have seen in my life and I counted because they were miracles by the universe, but some miracles happen every day in our life and need to just be observed.

Is it a miracle you have enough food to eat, when a lot of people suffer from malnutrition?

Is it a miracle you have enough water to drink, when lots of people do not even have water to drink?

Is it a miracle, that you are breathing fresh air, while many people are suffering from pollution?

Is it a miracle, that you are a well-educated person, while many people are illiterate

Is it a miracle, that you have enough money to meet all your needs, while people are doing hard work to hold onto their one day expense.

Is it a miracle you and your family are completely healthy, while some people have to continuously take rounds of hospitals

Is it a miracle you have your own house while some people sleep on the road,

Is it a miracle you have a big house, while some families sleep in one room?

Is it a miracle you have healthy hands, while some people work without hands

Is it a miracle you have both parents with you, while people don't have.

Is it a miracle that god gifts you a child, while many people are childless

Is it a miracle you have your own business, while people are working as servant

Is it a miracle you have a job, while many people are jobless

Is it a miracle you have money to buy your favourite things while some people have only for food.?

There are many little things you have, that other people do not have and it is a miracle or the blessing of the universe, which is given you for free. But the sad part is, that you never observe the blessing of the universe, while you complain about the universe you don't have. How you can expect another miracle in your life, while you do not count it or acknowledge it right now.

I am sharing the story of a lady, god gifted her everything good health, wealth, good business, big house, but still, she was never happy, she was not happy with what god had already gifted her. At her initial stage, she had nothing but god gifted her everything that she needed, to live a good life. But she always looked at others and always felt jealous emotions towards others, she was neither happy with her things nor with others. Whenever she met someone, she started to feel jealous by looking at their growth and happiness. After some time, she started to fall ill, her illness worsen,, along with her mental status and now she was not even able to enjoy what she already had because she was bed ridden because of the life-threatening disease she had. She went through many surgeries. She was still not able to recover because she attracted, what she said about others, she felt about others.

This story is a telling, that the lady was never happy in the present moment, never happy with what she already had, never happy with others, her negative thoughts for others became the truth of her life and she was never able to enjoy the gift of god already given to her due to life threatening disease. .

I hope you got my point, there are thousands of miracles already happening in your life, so feel blessed & happy by saying thank you for what you already have. Say positive words & think positive and be happy for your growth and abundance in your life.

Be grateful for everything and whatever situation you have right now. See everything as learning lesson from life if something is not working out. And be grounded and thankful to universe even you are getting success.

Loud every day in the morning about your self

I am so happy and blessed that I have this beautiful house

I am so happy and blessed that I have a healthy body

I am so happy and blessed that I have a wonderful job

I am so happy and blessed my business has good sales.

I am so grateful and blessed that every time I travelled safely.

I am so grateful that me and my family are safe all the time.

Always count your miracles or blessings that happen in the present every day or for the things you already have.

Whenever you count the miracles, feel happy and blessed to have, you can count any 15 things for which you are grateful the most.

You can make the list of things, situations you already have and you are grateful for that.

First you can start with any 5 things which is already present in your life, then after week you can increase it by 10 things in your counting, then to 15 things as part of daily ritual to be grateful for everything you have now in your consciousness.

WORDS HAVE POWER

Here, I want to share the power of words, whatever you say, again and again, will become the truth.

Because words have power, vibration, and frequency. Whatever you will say again and again will become the truth of your life.

Never think, that if you are saying negatives to others, it will hurt others, while saying negatives to others or using negative words with others you are making a circle of negativity around you, which will only hurt you .

 Never say or use negative words for yourself again and again even by mistake. Whatever you will say about yourself, you will create that negativity for you and you will be that. Your dominant thought will affect your mind, and your subconscious mind will read it and will make it a reality.

Have you ever seen any Rich man in the world, saying negative or taking negative about themselves or to others? They know the power of words; they use the power of words.

Most of the time, they use positive words, inspiring words, words for helping others, and words for growth, they are talking about success, and they are giving guidance for success.

They mostly use powerful words for themselves , they are mostly in a grateful state, they think about the growth of their employees, they think about their company's growth, and they sit only with positive people. They speak less and listen more or only needful. Whenever they speak, its only positive or for success or motivation.

Look at speeches of Mark Zuckerberg, Bill Gates, Mukesh Ambani, Ratan Tata, Jeff Bezos, Elon Musk

All the famous or rich people talk about the positive, success, and growth.

So, from today onwards whenever you speak, speak positively about your health, wealth, and relationships.

Whenever you speak about others always speak positively about their health, wealth, and relationships.

Here, I am talking about my father, since my childhood I saw my father always talk positively about his business, he was always in a grateful state for his business, I mostly saw him say, whatever we have by only god's grace. We are earning good by god's grace. All is good in our life by god's grace. These are the words I have mostly heard till now. And by god's grace business is running well and we are living a good life by god's grace.

Your 5 senses continuously, use the power of words, like speaking from your mouth, writing from your hand,, listening from you ear, seeing through your eyes, and by feeling. If you learn or can control yourself to avoid negative thoughts or people and will use these senses to see only the positive, to give only the positive, to think positively, to read only the positive, to listen positively, to feel only positive. Then soon you will be a more positive and a more successful person.

Because, all around you, words are moving, and they are so powerful. Because words generate feelings, feelings generate reality. Choose your words wisely while talking, listening, reading and writing.

WHAT YOUR EMOTION SPEAKS

As human body has 5 senses, hearing, tasting, touch, smell, and sight. By all these senses human body can feel the senses, these senses allow you to feel the emotions

Like, when **you touch** something you can feel what it is, but you can also feel what you feeling after touching it.

Same way, when you see something, you can see what it is with your eyes, but at the same time you will have some emotions like feeling good or bad, excited, amazing, happy, grateful, blessed, about particular thing.

Like when a mother sees her child's face for the first time, what emotions will come? She will feel blessed or grateful or thankful to god for a blessed healthy baby.

Another example, is when you see, a god idol in any temple or any of your gurus in front of you, what will you feel? You will feel emotional that you got the chance to meet him, you will feel blessed, you will feel grateful.

Whenever you get the outcome, which you want in your life, you will get positive emotions.

Like feeling blessed, thankful, grateful, happy, lucky, privileged, fortunate, abundant, rich, positive, good, excited, humbled, kind, loved, etc are the positive emotions.

These emotions will always connect you, to your supreme intelligence and soon you start to be satisfied with these things, and always lead you to achieve more. As the human mind is never satisfied.

Any guru or monk is never satisfied with their spiritual practice, because they feel more grateful in the spiritual practice. The more knowledge they gather, the more practice they do to achieve higher intelligence. But this universe is infinite, knowledge is infinite and supreme intelligence is infinite beyond our imagination.

Let's discuss negative emotions. Whenever you start any work or you want to achieve anything you will always be doubtful , as to whether it will work or not, what it is, how will you do it, how it will happen, it's not possible, I can't do it etc.. Soon you start to think negatively; more negative patterns will start to occur in your mind.

Like you preparing for any exam, you have emotions, like how will I do it, this subject is hard, how will I cover the syllabus, I didn't give some tests so I can't do it, because of the exam now you have emotions like fear, nervousness, anxiety, fear of failure.

Another example is when you prepare for an interview, where 3 to 6 people will take your interview, most of the emotions you have are nervousness, rejection, doubtful, hopelessness, insult, and criticized.

Another example is when you are in a relationship, but due to your insecurities, you start feeling emotions like not being loved, not being cared for, controlled, hurt, possessive etc. .

When you go to anyplace alone, where nobody is present, the emotions you will feel are , scared, fear, attacked.

When you get any negative news, your emotions will be like, shocked, shattered, hurt, painful, betrayed, etc.

These negative emotions will lower your frequency, and soon you will start to feel dull, lazy, low in energy, ill, not focused.

So, emotions are so powerful and directly connected to your supreme intelligence, which guides you after listening to your emotions and will give you the same command, whatever emotions you feel related to anything or any situation.

So, you need to be very careful or need to be aware of your emotions, and how you feeling now.

Because you are in the present, your life is in the present moment, whatever is around is present. And whatever emotion you will feel in the present, related to anything or any situation, you will attract the same more and more in your life.

So, check your list of emotions related to anything you have now, what emotions are you feeling?

If you want to attract abundance, goodness, good health, money, wealth, and prosperity, fame start feeling positive emotions more and more in your life by whatever you have right now or in the present moment, or today.

You can choose 3 areas of your life for feeling your emotions.

How do you feel about yourself and your health now?

How do you feel about your wealth now?

How do you feel about your family now?

If you have any memory related to these areas of your life, through which you feel negative, change the patterns of feeling emotions related to that situation or that thing. How you can change the pattern of your emotions I will tell you on the next topic of forgiveness.

Your task... from today onwards whatever you will do, will always have positive emotions, So now through your 5 senses, you always feel positive emotions like, thankful, grateful, blessed, energetic, peaceful, happy, loved, cared, etc.

Positive emotions will higher your frequency, higher your vibration, and connect you to your supreme intelligence. Consciously or subconsciously you will start feeling positive emotions for everything in your life or around you.

FORGIVENESS

Forgive, forget and forward are the keys to success

When I am talking about the word forgiveness, it's a positive emotion, which helps you to connect with your supreme intelligence power. Learn the art of forgiveness to someone or any situation or any memories. Learn the art of forgiving and accepting the forgiveness.

Here I am telling you some examples, of how you indulge in negative emotions when you do not forgive anyone or any situation.

If someone hurts you through their action by cheating on you, abusing you, or not supporting you, you start feeling resentment regarding the event, and you start imagining a picture of that event again & again in your mind, that how a person hurt you, and you are not ready to let go of the event or forgiving them by your mind.

Not forgiving someone, or forgiving someone just through words, will never give you mental peace, and you will feel the same negative emotions again and again. This will lower your vibration, and you will not be able to focus on things that are far better than that resentment.

Keep in mind, that god sent you here with some purpose, to find a purpose is to serve humanity, but you need to become a person, who can forgive the situation and any person.

What are other similar words of forgiveness? Excuse, quit, dispose of, leave, discard, or unchain.

It means you have to learn the art of unchaining, disposing off, or learning to leave that situation or person in your mind.

If you forgive someone with love, with intention, that now I am forgiving you for that…(event) with love and compassion, I wish happiness in your way. Now I am forgiving you from my great heart with love.

The same way you can write the same statement on blank paper or name of the person ... now I am forgiving you for…. (event).. with love and compassion, wish you always happy on your ways. Now you can tear that paper or you put fire on that and feel that letting things go forever. And say God is there to guide you, god is here to guide me.

Now write the statement ' Now I am happy with full of love and compassion , repeat this in mind with positive emotions and say now I am moving forward for the goodness of my life given by the universe.' And now say god is there to guide me.

The above statement will help you to forget things and helps you move forward in your life, as god already guided you to move forward through forgiveness with love, and will help you again to connect with your supreme intelligence with self-love.

Now look forward to things, start loving yourself, by saying positive about yourself, look at what is positive in you, through which god empowered you. I will teach you self-love in the next topic, which covers the art of selflove, through which you can connect to your supreme intelligence for your wellness.

After forgiving someone, you will now be more focused emotionally and intelligently on, what you want to do.

SELF-LOVE

Self-love, defining self-love means caring about your emotions, and embracing yourself to the fullest. Most people waste their time criticizing others, hating someone, wasting their time in jealousy and revenge, and creating negativity around them, as like attracts like and hate attracts hate, and they forget to embrace themselves and their lives. When you hate someone or are jealous of them, of your thoughts, words, and actions, soon start to create negativity for yourself. And due to negative emotions, your vibration start to become low. For manifesting desires in your life, you need to keep your vibrations high.

When you think negatively or speak negatively to others consciously, your subconscious mind does not differentiate the person, it only reads your emotions related to that person or incident. As per your emotions, it starts to give you the same result in your life and you may face negativity in your life because of that negative emotion. And that negativity may create your ill health

So, for high vibration, you need to always keep yourself happy in the present moment. For self-love starts with the practice of gratitude. Practicing gratitude will make you a kinder and happier person in your life and it creates magic in your life, you will be more peaceful and happy.

For practicing self-love, say positive things about yourself. Say loudly now Yes, I am a happy person, Yes, I am a kind person. Yes, I am worthy. Yes, I love myself, I love the people around me. Yes, I am beautiful, Yes, I am smart. Yes, I embrace my strengths and acknowledge my areas for growth. Whatever my strength, is my biggest power to improve myself. I am the person to whom people trust and acknowledge. I am a person with a happy heart. Saying positive things to yourself is the biggest form of self-love and care.

Learn to forgive and forget and move forward for your own happiness. Forgiveness will give you the strength get rid of resentment or negative emotions and will help to move forward for self-love.

Every day in the morning Start self-communication instead of others. Say loudly any 10 positive things about yourself. After that Create a mental picture of your attributes or whatever positive you are saying about yourself. Feel the emotions when you do this practice every morning. For instance, if you are saying.

I am confident. I am intelligent. I am a genius.

I am the best speaker. I am a good reader. I am the best sales man. I am doing my best in my job.

I am a positive person; I am a person full of love. I am a kind person. I am a grateful person.

I am energetic. I am a good family person. I am a good team leader.

I am a decision-maker. I am successful. I am abundant. I am rich, I am wealthy.

I love myself. People around me love me. My life is full of love and kindness.

I am healthy. My each cell is happy and healthy.

I take action about my goal. I make the plan, and I execute the my planning on time.

I am disciple person, I am following healthy routine

When you start saying first yourself **what you are**, you will become the same as what you said to yourself. Don't judge yourself when you are telling positive about yourself. Feel the emotion of love, happiness, peace, joy, blessed, thankfulness, and grateful for you. And see the miracle after 21 days of this practice.

Why are you waiting for someone, who praises you? First, you learn to praise yourself, learn to admire yourself with emotions of gratitude, love, and compassion. Feel the privilege to have a positive attitude in you. Give the command to your subconscious mind every morning, that you are grateful to have this now.

It should be a positive affirmation to yourself, in the present tense.

Now look, when a person says to you, you are a charming person, after listing your admiration, what are you feeling now? Now You feel wow, thank you for saying that to me, and now your subconscious mind has taken that command, that you are a charming person, and you start looking at yourself as a charming person. So, what's the difference between you and the other person saying the same statement to yourself?

The difference is that, when other people praises you, you feel as I am that person and you accept that as reality. But when you own, say the same words to yourself, you do not accept that, your conscious mind rejects that, you are not that. Why? Because your subconscious mind is trained for that, we should not self-praise. As your conscious mind receives the command of your statement, your subconscious mind will reject it.

So, learn to train your subconscious mind with powerful and positive words or statements every day in the morning and before bed about yourself. And surly, miracles will happen each day and will transform your life full of love, success, wealth, etc.

Self-love is what first you think about yourself. No matter what others think or say about you. Only what you think and say about yourself will be your reality. Only you will define your destiny, not someone else.

In any relationship, if you facing hardship, maybe you are the first person responsible for that. If you are not getting love and respect in return because you are not giving it first to others. First create the mental picture of giving love, care, support, and respect to others and receive the same in your mind. Do this practice every day with a feeling of love and care and blessed with whom you want

Self-Love

1. Say positive things to yourself every morning or before bed.
2. Practice every day self-praises with positive statements or words.

3. Learn to be quiet and more vocal to positive words.
4. Make the practice of expressing positive emotions from inside or outside.
5. Stop judging yourself by someone's statement or criticism.
6. Start doing what you love to do the most, find the best different thing you love to do and start any one, you are comfortable doing. And feel the emotion of love by doing that.
7. Maintain a healthy lifestyle by doing exercise, yoga or meditation, or a simple 30 min walk in your daily routine.
8. Read books for self-help.
9. Make a daily practice of getting up early in the morning and practicing gratitude for what you have now.
10. Start praising others for their goodness and achievement, or motivate others by your positive statement.

CLARITY OF THOUGHT AND BELIEF

If you want to see miracles in your life, your thoughts should be very clear. What do you exactly want in your life? If you don't have the clarity of things you want to manifest in your life, you will often feel the law of attraction not work. But the universe is working each moment for all of us. We all have the monkey mind, which jumps here & there all the time, and that's why we are not able to focus on what we want to do.

The best way to have clarity on what you exactly want in your life, or within 10 years or 5 years. You should have the clarity of time as well. Time plays an important role, in the physical form to achieve things in a certain time frame.

To have clarity of thought or goal, always use pen and paper, ask some questions to yourself, write the answer, and find the reason for that answer, why you want this.

Like

What do you want in the present moment in all these areas which I mentioned below?

We mostly focus on the things, that we don't want in our lives, and we attract the same. If we focus with clarity on what we want, which we also love and enjoy, we will attract the same.

So, if you want a new job or promotion, instead of saying of focusing that your current job is not good, they are not giving you enough money, it's a very tiring job, etc, will create a negative pattern in your mind by saying negative to your current job. Because before this job you had nothing. So instead of a negative thought, focus on what this job or business gives you with a positive statement.

Like you can say I am happy with my job and business. I am earning a good amount of money. I am fulfilling my dreams now with this money. I am truly grateful for the money which I am receiving as a salary or income because it keeps me and my family happy all the time. I love my business and job. I love my colleagues and boss who support me all the time. I love the sitting area where I am working comfortably. My clients and customers are happy with my service. They are getting value with my service. I am so happy and grateful now to have a wonderful job or business that I have now. My product or service sales are increasing every day. My customers are happy with my product and service.

So, all the positive statements, which I mentioned above which you can use for your current job or business. Repeating all the statements every morning and evening will higher your vibration regarding your career, and you will attract more abundance in your career.

Now after this practice, write it on paper and pen, what kind of job do you want? how much salary you want now, how many hours you want to work for that job you want, which place you want the job, and in which company you want the job, but be realistic to have skills or knowledge for that particular job profile.

For example, Mukesh is working as sales man now and he has 1 lakh salary per month. Now he made his next clear goal of having 5 lakh rupees per month salary in the year 2024 with the company name.

Goal- he made his next clear goal of having 5 lakh rupees per month salary in the year 2024 with the company name.

Why does he want this salary?

Because it will higher his living status and he will enjoy this salary to fulfil all the dreams he wants to fulfil in year 2024 with his family.

What he will do with this salary?

He will buy a new big house (Be Clear yourself what kind of house you want).

He will buy a car (clear which car he wants).

Debt-free (clear the amount of loan).

Buy the land for future investment. (Clear the area and place)

Travel

Insurance

Donation

You can write any 10 very important things, which you can do with this money, and the things you want with this money should be part of immense happiness. You have to be very clear about what exact thing you want, at which place, what time, what colour, what model, and to whom you will share that thing.

For example, you want to buy a new house with this money, so be clear about the place & society you want to buy a home or land. Clear the exact area you want in that place. How many rooms will be there? It can be 2bhk or 3bhk or 4bhk or 5bhk anything which you really want. Go in deep state and think as much as you can think, there is no limit. You can ask anything from the universe but it should be very clear, there should be no change after getting a clear picture of what you want. Now think of the exact colour of the inside or outside of the home, and get a detailed picture of each room in your mind. What kind of painting or colour, chairs, bed, or sofa do you want in your home? Even includes washroom and kitchen. Think about the first day of that home when you doing the inauguration ceremony with family and friends in that new home, think how you celebrated that day when you entered that home, how much you are grateful to god and universe for achieving that success or having that beautiful home. Add as many as details you want in that home, and have the exact clarity of things you want in that home. Also imagine that home is debt free and you feeling blessed for that.

You can make a list of things you want in that home, now whatever you think about your home in your mind write on a paper with a blue pen and read every morning or before bed and feel gratitude as much as possible for having that home now. And also feel gratitude for the home you currently living in.

So above example was for the home and you can add anything or a goal with the exact clarity you want.

Thank you god, for having now 4bhk penthouse in………(Society name) Ahmedabad in 2024.

Thank you, god, for having 6000 Sq ft agricultural land in (place) in (state) in (year).

Thank you, god, for having now 1 lakh Rs monthly salary or income in the year 2024.

Thank you, god for having a job now in ………….. (Company name) in (year).

Thank you, god, for having 3 lakh rs monthly sales through my business.

Thank you, god, for having now blue colour car (model number) in 2024.

Thank you God my child got admission in that school/college (name of school and college).

You can add any amount you want as salary or monthly or yearly income in your affirmations, but should be realistic for recent years. Will suggest you just double the amount for the start.

VISUALIZATION

Visualization is a very important step in manifestation or attracting things you want in your life. Often you can see, as you see any attractive thing or place , you are attracted more towards that and soon you feel that you want it. Why?

You are attracted more because you like it, you feel attached to it. You feel loved. And again, and again, you think and see the picture of that thing or place because you want this now in your life.

You can also observe that the food you love or your favourite food, and someone talking about the same, your mouth will be watery, why? Because you love it. When someone talked about the exact recipe you liked you soon start felt hungry for it. And felt a watery mouth. Because your mind already understands the taste of that recipe whenever you have eaten and praises in your mind, or gave the command to your mind that I love that thing or food.

So, in visualization, you can use creativity. Creativity will give you the sense of emotion of love and likeness towards that thing. You can use your 5 senses that are vision, touch, smell, hear, voice, or taste. Our 5 senses will help you to train your subconscious mind more effectively for the things you want in your life.

For example, you want a soul mate or want to attract a life partner in your life.

Think about you with your life partner, holding hands with each other, and think about the place where you are together (a place you already visited in your city would give you a clear picture). Praising each other, seeing yourself with love in each other eyes. Visualize the colour of the dress you both wearing now. Think this moment is now already happening. You feel loved, blessed, excited, happy, joyful, satisfaction in this moment. You are grateful to god or the universe for having this moment in your life with your life partner. You hear the voice of you and your partner saying something to each other. I love you or I liked you. You feel the touch of your partner with a sense of satisfaction and trust. You can visualize yourself with colour and the place where you are sitting together. You can smell the fragrance of the perfume you both are wearing.

You can also visualize a honeymoon place where both of you are together a place like a beach or a cruise or snow, and visualize the place you like the most with him or her. Visualize the surprise you have given to him or her. And he or she loved that surprise and say thank you to you. Feel your soul mate is happy with you, in love with you, attached to you, and feeling blessed with you. He or she loved it when you were with them. Feel you are the perfect partner the exact one he or she wants in your life.

Add more and more creativity to things you want in your life.

You can also use a vision board. Keep that in your bedroom and see it every morning as soon you get up and before bed when you go to sleep. Add the cut-out of colourful pictures of things you want in your life.

Add cut-out of emotion quotes that you will feel when the things you have it. Add the Year in which you want the things. Add positive affirmation for particular things. Add a money picture with the exact amount to fulfil that desire. Add things to the vision board with clarity. I would suggest spending 10 min in front of the vision board every day and feel that you already have and you are grateful for all these things.

You can start visualization practice with any small object you have and visualize that object 5 times in your mind every 2 min. Open your eyes see that object, close your eyes see that object in your mind, and feel you are with that object with love and gratitude. Again, open your eyes and see that object clearly in the present, and now again close your eyes and see that object in your mind in the present you are with that, with detail picture of the event in your mind with that object.

Even you can visualize any situation same way in your mind. Be clear as much as you want that situation. Like, if you are going for any meeting or interview. Both are situations, so before going to any meeting or interview visualize the situation that you cleared the interview and now you are so happy, see yourself to be happy, see yourself, that you are saying thank you to god, see yourself you sharing this happiness with your one family member, visualize his or her face, they are congratulating for this. Same way you can visualize the successful meeting, and how you celebrate that Successful meeting with gratitude, emotion, and feelings.

One important step is, first make an action plan of what major action you are going to take for your goal, you can make a flow chart of your action plan for achieving that goal. Write your action plan with clear words about what important step is required to achieve that goal or thing. Now visualize each action or step you are going to take till then you finally take action, then visualize the next action or step towards your goal. With this practice, you will finally be able to take action in reality.

FOLLOWINGS

1. *Visualisations Works For Those Who Believe In Miracles*
2. *Visualization Works For Those Who Believe Yes, You Have Now.*
3. *Visualization Is A Process To Create Miracles*
4. *Visualization Works With Consistent Practice.*
5. *Visualization Works With What You See Inside Or Outside.*
6. *Visualize First With Clarity And What You Love And Want Now.*

ONE SHLOKA FROM HINDU GRANTHA " YAT PINDE TAT BRAMANDE" MEANS WHATEVER YOU SEE INSIDE IS OUTSIDE IN THE UNIVERSE, & WHATEVER YOU SEE OUTSIDE IS IN INSIDE YOU.

SO, WHATEVER YOU WILL SEE INSIDE THAT WILL BE MANIFEST IN REALITY IN FRONT OF YOUR EYES IN YOUR LIFE.

LET'S CREATE THE MIRACLES

Count the miracles and be grateful with feelings whatever you have now. Look around you, people, things, situations, health, body, mind, soul, nature, relationship, food, water, air, earth, whatever you have now you can see, you can feel, you can hear, you can touch, be grateful for all these things.

You can start with **any 5 things you have now**, and be grateful as much as possible to have now in the present moment. Think about what you are grateful for, why you are grateful, and what you are getting with this now.

You can increase the list as per practice.

Example

Thank you, God, I am truly grateful for the **fresh Air,** I am breathing now, it's keeping my body alive now and it's giving life to each cell of mine and keeping it healthy now.

Thank you, god, I am truly grateful for me and my family's good health, which gives me and my family peace of mind, I am feeling abundant and blessed to have a healthy and happy life now.

Thank you, god, I am truly grateful for the people around me who love me, care about me and always support me, I can see each face of people who are more important to me and support me unconditionally in every situation. Wherever I am, people love my vibes and are happy with me.

Thank you, god, I am truly grateful, that I have a powerful soul, I am worthy, I am confident, I am an action taker, I am a decision maker, and I love whatever I am doing now. It makes me happy and abundant now.

Thank you, god, I am so grateful for the amount of money, that I invested in mine and my family's happiness. I am blessed now that money is flowing and increasing every day in my life , I am happy and peaceful with that money, and living life with this money purposefully. I am grateful that I have money to help others for good deeds, which increases my good karma.

So, count the miracles or blessings already given by the god by saying thank you with feelings.

You can start this gratitude practice early in the morning when you just awaken.

1. **Gratitude Practice (Count Your Miracles)**

Exp- Thank you god I am so grateful to have this beautiful home. I am living so happily and peacefully in this beautiful home.

2. **Powerful words (Speak 10 positive statements in present tense)**

Exp- I am confident now

I am rich now

I am healthy now

3. Focus on your positive emotions

Every day in the morning and evening before sleeping focus on your positive emotions and feel that emotion.

Exp- Today I am full of love with my family visualize it.

Today I am happy

Today I am blessed

Today I am peaceful.

4. Learn to forgive.

Learn to forgive someone, it will relax your mind, and give you peace of mind

Practice of forgiving someone will increase your positive vibration, after forgiving someone you will be able to forget the situation, and move forward in your life.

You will be more focused on your present life or present goal.

Learn to maintain distance not only physically but also mentally by forgiving someone, and now focused on your personal growth.

5. Self-Love

Learn to care about your emotions and feelings by Self-communication, Close your eyes and communicate yourself with feelings and words with positive statements. Keep yourself full of love, happiness, and kindness.

6. Clarity of Thought and Belief

Be clear about your present life, how exactly do you want to live your life now?

Be clear about goals in all areas of life.

Be clear about your monthly and yearly goal.

Be clear about what things exactly you want now.

Your every thought should be clear.

What kind of belief do you have now?

What kind of belief you should have in the situation you want now?

What kind of belief do you have now for your goal?

Do you know exactly what things you are going to do today?

What is your belief about your present situation?

What kind of belief do you have now for your health?

Most people in this world are not clear about what exactly they want in their life, or what exactly their purpose is in this life. They just live their life to earn, eat, and sleep. The person who is already clear about what exactly they want in their life, they manifest it easily in their life. Clarity gives the imagination of particular thing or situation happening in your life and clarity increases the focus for that particular thing you want in your life. We can understand it with the example.

Suppose one person wants to visit 7 wonders, that is his goal.

But he has to be very clear about which wonders he wants to visit first, and in which country that one wonder is present. Which state or city of that country, wonder is present? How's the structure of that wonder? Why it's inspiring you to visit, what's the story behind it? All these details will give you clarity about the place you want to visit. How you will reach there, how you will travel for that place to visit, what amount of money exactly you want to visit that place for that great memory in your life.

(All these details will give you a clear picture of visiting that place, when you work on that you will create a visualization process in your mind with emotions that, will help you manifest it in reality).

Belief system works on emotions you have for particular things.

Another example suppose **one person wants to become a chess champion in the year 2024.**

He or she has to be very clear that he loves to play chess and enjoys playing chess, he has to be very clear about his practice that every day 2 hrs or 3 hrs or whatever is required, he or she will invest in the practice of playing chess. He or she has to be clear about the coach from whom he is going to take coaching. What tournament is coming this year, which particular tournament does he want to participate in?

If you want to earn any large money, you have to be very clear, about exactly how much amount of money you want monthly, quarterly or yearly basis. So, write the exact amount you want. Also be clear about what you are going to do with this amount. Why do you want this amount. Which problem in your life will be solved by this income? What things do you want to buy with this money? Which place you will visit with this money? You have to be very clear about each thing you will buy with this money.

BELIEF

After getting clarity of things you want in your life, you need to believe yes you can achieve that. Belief confirms the event that it's 100 % going to happen. So, if you want to attract the miracles in your life you have to believe in miracles in your life.

It doesn't matter how much your prayer is good. But your prayer works only by the power of belief. You have to be ensured that whatever you are asking in your prayer to God or the universe is 100% already solved and that is belief.

You have to imagine in your mind that it has already happened and been solved by the god or universe and you are grateful for that. You have emotions of thankfulness, happiness, blessedness, and gratefulness for that moment that you want already happened.

So firstly, work on your emotions in your mind each day. What kind of emotions do you have right now in your mind? Make a list of that. Ask yourself, are these positive emotions or negative emotions?

If your emotions are negative for any person or for any situation you want in your life, and you again & again keep that negative emotion in your mind, you giving 100 % belief to your mind that it's already happened.

And each day your situation gets worse, because of your negative belief about yourself or your situation.

So, let's learn to change your beliefs about yourself or your particular situation. **How you can change your belief?**

Forgiveness will create positivity around you and let go of things there're on way. You will feel more relaxed, calm, and peaceful. And after forgiving someone you can move forward in your life to attract abundance and for the life you want.

Self-doubt –If you have self-doubt that you can't do it, I can't achieve it, I am not worthy, I can't become, I can't hold, I can't be successful, by these negative statements of self-doubt, you will not be able to achieve what you desire. So, stop repeating these statements in your mind or by speaking with words. Change the self-doubt perceptions. And convert it in a positive statement.

Negative belief	**Positive belief**
I can't do it	I can do it now
I can't achieve it	I can achieve it now
I can't become	I can become now
I am not good	I am good now
I am not beautiful	I am beautiful now
I am not intelligent	I am intelligent now
Nobody loves me	People around me love me now
I am not rich	Yes, I am Rich now
I am not healthy	I am healthy & happy now

If you facing any negative situation change your mindset for that situation or person with a positive statement. Do this practice in your mind with positive emotions for 21 days, at the time when you just wake up or just fall asleep at night. You can also practice it at the time when you feel peaceful and relaxed.

After practicing it you can see changes or miracles in your life by improving your situation day by day. And your belief will convert from a negative to a positive situation.

You also need to ensure what kind of company you have now, what they suggesting you, what is their thinking pattern , and what kind of talk they have with you on a daily basis. What kind of thoughts do they have for money and business? They have a growth mind set or not. What they are doing now for their growth. What kind of lifestyle do they have now? Do they have limiting beliefs?

A rotten apple gets also rot other apples around it. But if an apple is fresh will keep other apples fresh long time. So, it's matters what kind of company you have now. If you have company of people who do not inspire you for your growth then defiantly it will ruin your life.

They should inspiring you.

They should motivate you.

They should speak positively to you.

Negative company	**Good Company**
Don't do this	You should try to learn it
This will happen (assumption)	Take the risk
Fearful	decision maker

No learning abilities	learning abilities
Limiting belief	Growth mind-set
Compromise	Achiever
Negative thought	Positive thought
Speak negative	Speak positive
Delays	discipline
Excuses	Action mode
Small thinking	Big goal
Adjust to lifestyle	Create a life style
Lack of reading skills	Read inspiring books
Fault finder	improves the situation
Criticising	kind and loving

Choose comfortable zone big goal maker

So, look around you and what kind of people are around you. If you can't change your company then become a silent person, speak less with them, and listen less to them. Make good company by reading self-help books or inspiring books, reading these books daily, will change your limiting or negative beliefs into positive beliefs.

What kind of belief do you have for yourself, look at yourself or look at the list given above. Think about which company you belong to. Give a true remark to yourself to change your belief. If not in good company list it's ok now. Change your mindset now, and start believing that you belong to a good company now start reading inspiring, growth mindset books which turn your life to become a good and successful person, who can inspire others.

7. **Forgiveness- learn to give forgiveness to others or situations or yourself.**

Affirmation practice – **Affirmation practice will transform your life miraculously**

WHAT you affirm for yourself or the strong statement you give for yourself will become your reality.

Whatever you are saying, for yourself or others your mind is listening to you 24x7 all the time. If you will affirm negative for yourself or for others it will create negativity in your life, It does not harm others it will harm you first. So, beware of talking negative. Because you train your mind each day by your thoughts, emotions, and beliefs.

So, start practicing writing positive affirmations or speaking the affirmation while meditating or randomly speaking daily. You can make your affirmation as per your priorities or choices. But you have to practice it daily.

Daily practice of positive affirmation will strengthen your belief in your situation and transform your life miraculously.

Now do daily practice of positive affirmations regarding 3 main areas of your life.

Health – Thank you god I am so grateful now that I and my family are completely healthy, happy, and living a peaceful life. Thank you for keeping us safe all the time.

(Thank you, god, I am healthy and happy now)

Wealth- Thank you god I am so blessed now that abundance freely flowing in my life attracting opportunities in my life and giving me financial abundance.

(Thank you, god, for all the financial abundance)

Relationship- Thank you god I am blessed to have all the loving relationships around me. People love me care for me and support me all the time.

(Thank you, god, for I have good personal and professional relationships with people around me.

If you want to transform your life, work on your 5 senses,

What you are seeing

What you are listening

What you are speaking

What you are smelling

What you are touching

All these senses generate feelings, feelings create vibration and vibration creates frequency, and frequency creates life and reality.

Everything in the universe are made by small molecules called atoms, atoms vibrating at certain frequencies and these frequencies creating energy and that energy is your reality. So, our thoughts, feelings, and words are each made by energy and creating vibration.

So, if you want to attract something in your life, you have to create a similar vibration or frequency in your mind to match it in reality.

This universe is infinite and ready to give you infinite, but you need to ask yes you want this in your life, so start thinking big as much as you can, there is no limit to thinking big and achieving it. You can achieve it by creating a similar vibration in your mind by your strong or dominant thought for that particular thing.

Whatever you want to achieve, look around you and what is best in you, through which you can achieve all these things you want in your life. Do best what you know, grow it daily, and update yourself with the new version of yourself. Start taking small actions on things you want to do or love to do. Improve yourself by learning new skills. Take a risk in gratitude mode. Look at your goals daily to inspire you to achieve them, take action in mind first then take it in reality. Create your desirable outcome first in your mind then will happen in reality. If you fail don't worry, try again and again and again. Don't stop yourself by your silly excuse that I don't have or I can do it.

Still, if you do not succeed, then try other things but don't stop yourself from achieving your dreams and goals. First, focus on your big goal and then take small actions each day towards your goal.

And a miracle will happen and your goal will be a reality.

A man having a job with a monthly salary of 50 thousand cannot get 5 lakh rupees monthly salary.

Change your belief

Yes, you can get 5 lakh rupees monthly salary. Just think in your mind every day that now you have 5 lakh rupees monthly salary and you receive those 5 lakh rupees each month in your account and you are happy with that. Think each morning when you get up and when you fall asleep at night. Visualize it, feel it, affirm it in the present moment. And see the transformation after some months. Take action on how you can get 5 lakh rupees monthly salary. By job change or adding new skills. What change will happen in your life, what your dream be fulfilled by this income? By continuous practice you can see transformation in your life.

I am not worthy I cannot have a loving relationship; my relationship is not working.

Change your belief

I am a worthy person, I am a lovable person, and people around me love me and care about me. I deserve a lovable relationship. I know my life has wonderful lovable life partner for me. I am with the person who loves me and is my life partner. I am worthy of my life partner. I am with my soulmate and my soulmate is with me. We living our happy life together. My life partner has a loving and peaceful soul who loves me. We are traveling or visiting places together we loved. Start taking action for your life partner search, affirm a positive statement for yourself and to your life partner feel it, and visualize it in the present moment. And after some months you see a transformation in your life. feel the love for yourself and others will attract the loving relationship in your life. Most importantly you can find good relationship in any time there is no age group for that.

You can change your belief for any situation in your life and see the miracles by changing in your life, you can use them in your health, business, money, relationships, writing, speaking, reading, making anything in any situation. Change your belief from negative to positive and positive to more positive for moving on and seeing the miracles

A STORY.

A 15-year-old boy was very poor, not having sufficient food to eat, clothes to wear, and home to live in. And have money to spend to learn the things or buy the things. He was just surviving his life. One day he was just sitting in front of a luxurious hotel which was just near a beach. He saw many luxurious cars coming into the hotel and many rich people going into that hotel. He is much attracted by seeing that moment, how people are rich and enjoying their life in luxury.

After seeing that event the boy decides in his mind, he will also be rich one day and will enjoy his life similarly to rich people. He was thinking again and again in his mind to become rich. After several months of thinking he once again visited the same hotel from outside and once again he saw the same event, many rich people were coming into the hotel and enjoying the luxury. Not only did he clear his mind he was definitely going to rich one day and visit the same hotel the same way as other rich people. He visualizes himself that he is also rich now entering in same hotel as other rich people and enjoying a luxurious life. But it was only a dream, which he saw every day and that dream inspired to him think again and again about becoming rich. He visualizes himself that he is rich now and has a luxury home to live luxury car in which he is traveling. As soon as he wakes up from his dream, he realizes what he should do to become rich and a lot of money.

So, one day he got an offer to do labour work for a builder project. He was happy as he would get 500rs per day for this labour work. He was very happy and grateful for the 500rs now, because this money will bring happiness to his life. He thought one day when I will become so rich I would have a lot money and I would be happy same like today and He started working as a labourer in that project. After some time, as he was a talented boy his manager appointed him as labour manager, as due to some urgency the labour manager had to leave that job so he appointed him on a temporary basis. He was now handling 200 labourers on the project as a labour project. So, with handling labour he also started learning to arrange the vendors for the requirement of the materials used in that project.

As he was a very kind person people on that project liked him very much, so usually at lunchtime he started asking questions to senior managers, how we start any project if you have land. Now he learned so many things from the senior manager for handling any building project.

Soon he got an offer for making a bungalow of a rich person, he again got an offer as assistant manager for handling that project and he handled all that project on his own. This project was a game changer for him because he now understood the whole process of making any building and managing that.

Now he started looking so many other projects and sharing his previous experience for the next project. Now he was earning good, but it was not enough money through which he could live his luxury life which he was visualizing every day. So he was more curious about the big opportunity and he was searching for the big opportunity that will make him rich and fulfill all his dreams.

So now he met with a person who wanted to sell his agricultural land which was just near to the city. So now he suggested to the landowner if you will make building on this land, you will get more money than the selling price. The farmer got ready to make a building on this, but now he asked I didn't have the money to make the building, so the boy said, I will arrange that person who will invest his money in that. So, he just called that bungalow owner to invest money in that project and that bungalow owner arranged the investor for that building. So now, for the first-time boy got the chance to handing project as a builder and managing the whole building project was in his hand. After completing this project, the boy become the RICH at the age of 30, now he is the owner of a luxury car in which he want to travel, and now he has a big bungalow to live, a huge amount of money in his accounts, having luxury lifestyle and now he is more frequently visiting his dream hotels with his luxury car and enjoying the life he wants to enjoy which he was visualizing each day in his mind. He already lived that life in his mind, and that now happened in reality.

So never stop thinking big, finding opportunities, never stop taking risks, taking small and big actions, and belief in yourself. Believe in whatever you want in your life, and believe that things you have now in your mind and you are enjoying your life with those things. Clear in your mind that moment already happened in your life and you are enjoying that.

So, miracles happened in his life the same way it can happen in your life. Start thinking big, and erase self-doubt. Believe that it will surely happen. Clear the picture in your mind that it already happened and you are happy now and take action, find the opportunity, and don't stop till then you will not achieve your goal.

"One can only manifest his or her dream life by thinking big, finding opportunities, having clear goals, positive mindset and taking risks capabilities , knowing that the next steps will lead towards his or her goals."

"Create the mental picture every day in your mind of the life you want. Think you are abundant rich and a happy person."

"Think every day in your mind that your income and salary growing. You are receiving money effortlessly. Money is flowing easily in your life and you are thankful for that."

"Think every day in your mind that you have a loving relationship with your partner. Your partner respects you and you also respect him or her. You have a happy family."

"Think every day that you already have achieved your goals, your life and life style has changed and you are grateful for that too. . Be clear about your goals."

"Think every day in your mind and be grateful for your good health. Be grateful for having a healthy family, having healthy body and mind."

"Whatever you can see now with your eyes, whatever you can touch, whatever you can feel, be grateful now for that."

"Universe is within you, ask first in your mind, create first in your mind, achieve first in your mind, enjoy first in your mind, feel first in your mind and then see your reality with open eyes."

How a lady manifested dream trip to Kashmir.

One day a lady saw her friend's picture as they had recently visited Kashmir. As soon she saw the pictures of Kashmir, she was attracted towards the place. Soon, she started to see more videos of the Kashmir trip. Then she finally decided that she will go on a Kashmir trip with her family. Whenever she saw a video of Kashmir, she felt as if she was in Kashmir now and seeing all the sights in reality. It was a great attraction so everyday she saw the videos of Kashmir and felt that she was there in reality. One day she called up her another friend and asked to go on a Kashmir trip. She started calling travel agents to arrange the trip. Soon, she got to know that the trip's expense was 1.5 lakh. She had no idea from where she will arrange that money. As she had recently bought her new house. But by god's grace, she received money in her account from her PF account. And the amount was unexpected. The amount which she was expecting to receive from PF, was much more than that, it was exactly 1.5 lakh more.

She had already calculated the amount, but it was more than that, as she had missed the interest amount in calculation. And she received the amount with interest and that was exactly 1.5 lakh.

When she received the extra amount, she was so thankful to god and the universe. And then she visited Kashmir and fulfilled his dream of Kashmir. And it is a real story which I am sharing with you.

This story of how visualization works in the process of manifestation.

Another instance of how a man manifested his dream Job.

One man was looking for his dream job. He was very clear that he wanted a job which was part time. No load of work, minimum travelling and clear amount of salary. He started looking himself doing work from home, and receiving same amount salary in his account. Whenever he'd think and visualize the same, he would feel so happy and thankful to be doing this job, as he wanted the same job. Soon he got an offer of the same profile job which he was looking for. He was so happy to receive that same job.

How one girl manifested her dream life partner.

A girl wanted to get married but she was not getting the right partner. The reason behind that, she often meet any person she started looking, what's the lack in him. And it had become a habit to find faults in the person and saying that he was not her match. So she always ended up attracting the same person which was not her type. She was now totally frustrated as her subconscious mind had been trained for attracting the person which was not her match or whom she didn't want.

Because she often repeated, 'I don't want that type or this type of person.' Whenever she met the person, the negatively trained mind automatically started finding faults in that guy.

Because of that she even started losing good people from her life as she was focusing on finding faults.

Once, she cried and asked her friend, 'what is happening with me? Is nobody in the world for my type or good match for me, for marriage?' Soon, her friend suggested a manifestation coach who could help in to attract or manifest her life partner. Soon she visited that coach, who guided her to remove the blockages, to remove the negative mindset which she was holding onto in her mind. After taking training of changing mindset, she started thinking positively about her present state. She started thinking about self-love. She started looking at positive things in others. She started thinking good about marriage. So, whenever she met a new person, she would first focus on what's good in him. Soon she attracted her perfect match due to the change in mindset. She is happily married now.

So, it's all about what you think and feel you will attract. We mostly think what we don't want and forget about what we want.

If you want love in your life, start loving yourself first. Start finding love in others, focus on who loves you, cares for you, it feels like, 'Yes I am with the person who loves me cares for me, support me. I am thankful to the universe for providing a loving, supporting and caring life partner. Thank you, God.'

As soon you will affirm the same on a daily basis, your sub-conscious mind will attract the same. But you need to practice it on daily basis.

How one couple was saved from divorce.

I got a call from a lady who was cheated on by her husband. She started living separately from her husband and was suspicious of him. She was continuously thinking that her husband was cheating on her. She even made the image that how her husband had cheated her. When I asked her, 'did you catch him?' She said 'no' and then added, 'but I know he is cheating on me.'

I asked her, firstly to clear her negative beliefs on her husband that he was cheating on her, if she had not caught him red handed. Because she was training her mind about negative beliefs and not look at what was good in her relationship. How much her husband loved and cared for her.

Focus on good relationship. Focus on how much you both love each other and take care. After changing her belief with practice she start missing her husband. She remembered, how happily they both lived together. And soon she shifted back to her own home. And start living happily with her husband and family.

What's your belief, it may become your reality.

How a poor man became rich and a millionaire—a true story.

A man who belongs to a poor household and is only an 8th grade student, has so much responsibility. He was working at someone's house, they were too rich.. That man was mindful. After working at a rich family's house he decided that one day he will become rich. He started imaging himself as a rich person and that he could buy each thing which he loved. He started imagining having a big house, his dream house. And one day he converted that house in a reality. He imagined his child would be educated and well, its happened in reality. He decided clearly that he will live a debt free life, and he lived it. He does each and everything without any debt. He decided clearly how he will do his child's marriage and he did it in the same way. He decided how he will live his life and he is living in the same way. Now he is rich and a well settled person and doing well in his life.

It's up to you how you see yourself. How you design your life. What you think about yourself. If you think you are rich you will be rich, if you think you are happy you will be happy. Things matter what clearly you think about yourself.

Magic happens every Day, learn to design your life and become the magician of your life to create magic in your life. You can achieve or manifest whatever or anything you want or you love.

The author Ruchi Rai is life coach and the mindset coach, conducting several online courses or customize courses, live seminar on manifestation, law of attraction and numerology

www.ingramcontent.com/pod-product-compliance
Lightning Source LLC
LaVergne TN
LVHW041222080526
838199LV00082B/1917